Food and Drink
A Book of Quotations

EDITED BY

SUSAN L. RATTINER

DOVER PUBLICATIONS, INC.
Mineola, New York

DOVER THRIFT EDITIONS

GENERAL EDITOR: PAUL NEGRI
EDITOR OF THIS VOLUME: SUSAN L. RATTINER

*This book is dedicated to
all those who enjoy a good meal.*

Copyright

Copyright © 2002 by Dover Publications, Inc.
All rights reserved.

Bibliographical Note

Food and Drink: A Book of Quotations is a new work, first published by Dover Publications, Inc., in 2002.

Library of Congress Cataloging-in-Publication Data

Food and drink : a book of quotations / edited by Susan L. Rattiner.
p. cm. — (Dover thrift editions)
ISBN-13: 978-0-486-42209-1
ISBN-10: 0-486-42209-7 (pbk.)

1. Food—Quotations, maxims, etc. 2. Beverages—Quotations, maxims, etc. I. Rattiner, Susan L. II. Series.

PN6084.F6 F645 2002
641—dc21

2002018897

Manufactured in the United States by Courier Corporation
42209702
www.doverpublications.com

Note

*The majority of those who put together collections of verses
or epigrams resemble those who eat cherries or oysters; they
begin by choosing the best and end by eating everything.*

NICOLAS DE CHAMFORT (1741–1794)

SO MUCH OF our daily lives revolves around food: where we will eat,
what we will eat, how it will be prepared, what we should do about leftovers, and what we will eat tomorrow, or the next day—or even next
week. This obsession with food and drink spans the bounds of time and
culture. Even early humans were consumed with a passion for food,
since food has always meant survival. In ancient times, hunting and
gathering were full-time vocations that ultimately provided sustenance
for a family or village. However, the quest to find enough food to survive was not always successful.

Now that food and drink are relatively abundant in most parts of
today's world, their significance in pleasurable social rituals is greater
than ever before. The joy we share when gathering at a table with
friends and family is a literal feast for the soul. A skillful cook, a variety
of dishes, and a keen appetite are all an integral part of the complete
dining experience. *What* we eat is also important: there are comfort
foods that remind us of better times, fast food, vegetarian foods,
gourmet foods that tempt us with an exotic flair, and hearty, meat-and-
potatoes fare. A celebration of the strong connection between food and
life, this book of humorous and historical quotations offers traditional
proverbs from around the world, well-meaning advice from cooks and
writers, and diverse opinions on such topics as cooking, dieting, and
eating. This tantalizing array of wisdom and witticisms is a savory treat
for anyone who loves food and drink.

Contents

Contents

BREAKFAST, LUNCH, AND DINNER

When my mother had to get dinner for 8 she'd just make enough for 16 and only serve half.

GRACIE ALLEN

Never work before breakfast; if you have to work before breakfast, eat your breakfast first.

JOSH BILLINGS

In due time the tea was spread forth in handsome style; and neither ham, tarts, nor marmalade were wanting among its accompaniments.

CHARLOTTE BRONTË

A good breakfast is no substitute for a large dinner.

When going to an eating house, go to one that is filled with customers.

CHINESE PROVERB

Eat breakfast like a king, lunch like a prince, and dinner like a pauper.

ADELLE DAVIS

1

One can say everything best over a meal.

GEORGE ELIOT

We should look for someone to eat and drink with before look-ing for something to eat and drink, for dining alone is leading the life of a lion or wolf.

EPICURUS

He that waits upon fortune, is never sure of a dinner.

BENJAMIN FRANKLIN

It isn't so much what's on the table that matters, as what's on the chairs.

W. S. GILBERT

All happiness depends on a leisurely breakfast.

JOHN GUNTHER

Life, within doors, has few pleasanter prospects than a neatly arranged and well-provisioned breakfast table.

NATHANIEL HAWTHORNE

The kind man feeds his cat before sitting down to dinner.

HEBREW PROVERB

Nearly everyone wants at least one outstanding meal a day.

DUNCAN HINES

The American does not drink at meals as a sensible man should. Indeed, he has no meals. He stuffs for ten minutes thrice a day.

RUDYARD KIPLING

Oh, the pleasure of eating my dinner alone!

CHARLES LAMB

The dinner table is the center for the teaching and practicing not just of table manners but of conversation, consideration, tolerance, family feeling, and just about all the other accomplishments of polite society except the minuet.

JUDITH MARTIN, "MISS MANNERS"

Dinner, a time when . . . one should eat wisely but not too well, and talk well but not too wisely.

W. SOMERSET MAUGHAM

They sat down to tables that well might have groaned, even howled, such was the weight that they carried.

MARTHA McCULLOCH-WILLIAMS

There are a lot of people who must have the table laid in the usual fashion or they will not enjoy the dinner.

CHRISTOPHER MORLEY

The golden rule when reading the menu is, if you cannot pronounce it, you cannot afford it.

FRANK MUIR

Dinnertime is the most wonderful period of the day and perhaps its goal—the blossoming of the day. Breakfast is the bud.

NOVALIS

❖

Strange to see how a good dinner and feasting reconciles everybody.

SAMUEL PEPYS

❖

Great restaurants are, of course, nothing but mouth-brothels.

FREDERIC RAPHAEL

❖

Sit down and feed, and welcome to our table.

Unquiet meals make ill digestions.

And men sit down to that nourishment which is called supper.

WILLIAM SHAKESPEARE

❖

The hour of dinner includes everything of sensual and intellectual gratification which a great nation glories in producing.

SYDNEY SMITH

❖

A clear soup, a bit of fish, a couple of little entrées and a nice little roast. That's my kind of a dinner.

WILLIAM MAKEPEACE THACKERAY

They take great pride in making their dinner cost much; I take my pride in making my dinner cost little.

I sat at a table where were rich food and wine in abundance, and obsequious attendance, but sincerity and truth were not; and I went away hungry from the inhospitable board.

HENRY DAVID THOREAU

I went to dinner, which was served in a small private room of the club with the usual piano and fiddlers present to make conversation difficult and comfort impossible.

MARK TWAIN

My doctor told me to stop having intimate dinners for four. Unless there are three other people.

ORSON WELLES

Never argue at the dinner table, for the one who is not hungry gets the best of the argument.

RICHARD WHATELY

One cannot think well, love well, sleep well, if one has not dined well.

VIRGINIA WOOLF

Dining is and always was a great artistic opportunity.

FRANK LLOYD WRIGHT

COFFEE, TEA, AND OTHER BEVERAGES

Without my morning coffee I'm just like a dried up piece of roast goat.

JOHANN SEBASTIAN BACH

Coffee falls into the stomach [and] ideas begin to move, things remembered arrive at full gallop [and] the shafts of wit start up like sharp-shooters, similes arrive, the paper is covered with ink.

HONORÉ DE BALZAC

❖

No coffee can be good in the mouth that does not first send a sweet offering of odor to the nostrils.

HENRY WARD BEECHER

❖

POTABLE, n. Suitable for drinking. Water is said to be potable; indeed, some declare it our natural beverage, although even they find it palatable only when suffering from the recurrent disorder known as thirst, for which it is a medicine.

AMBROSE BIERCE

❖

The best wine is the oldest, the best water the newest.

WILLIAM BLAKE

❖

Never accept a drink from a urologist.

ERMA BOMBECK

There isn't enough coffee in the United States to keep everyone awake during a Presidential election campaign.

DONALD W. BROWN

There are various theories as to what characteristics, what combination of traits, what qualities in our men won [World War II] . . . but, speaking from my own observation of our armed forces, I should say the war was won on coffee.

ILKA CHASE

Better to be deprived of food for three days, than tea for one.

CHINESE PROVERB

❖

Never drink black coffee at lunch; it will keep you awake in the afternoon.

JILLY COOPER

❖

Coffee has two virtues: It is wet and warm.

DUTCH PROVERB

❖

Iced tea is too pure and natural a creation not to have been invented as soon as tea, ice, and hot weather crossed paths.

JOHN EGERTON

❖

These angry zombies were rushing to work, and their eyes flashed fair warning: *Don't mess with us. We haven't had our coffee.*

JOAN FRANK

❖

Coffee in England is just toasted milk.

CHRISTOPHER FRY

❖

Coffee was a food in that house, not a drink.

PATRICIA HAMPL

❖

The morning cup of coffee has an exhilaration about it which the cheering influence of the afternoon or evening cup of tea cannot be expected to reproduce.

OLIVER WENDELL HOLMES

No matter how much strong coffee we drink, almost any after-dinner speech will counteract it.

KIN HUBBARD

❖

I judge a restaurant by the bread and by the coffee.

BURT LANCASTER

❖

If this is coffee, please bring me some tea; but if this is tea, please bring me some coffee.

ABRAHAM LINCOLN

❖

The coffee was so strong it snarled as it lurched out of the pot.

BETTY MACDONALD

❖

Good to the last drop.

TEDDY ROOSEVELT

❖

Vodka is cursed, tea is twice cursed, coffee and tobacco are thrice cursed.

RUSSIAN PROVERB

Why do they always put mud into coffee on board steamers? Why does the tea generally taste of boiled boots?

WILLIAM MAKEPEACE THACKERAY

Water is the only drink for a wise man.

HENRY DAVID THOREAU

Coffee should be black as hell, strong as death, sweet as love.

TURKISH PROVERB

❖

It is inferior for coffee, but it is a pretty fair tea.

MARK TWAIN

❖

Tea to the English is really a picnic indoors.

ALICE WALKER

❖

And, upon my word, the very thing my soul was longing for—a cup of coffee!

MRS. HUMPHRY WARD

❖

Tea tempers the spirit, harmonizes the mind, dispels lassitude and relieves fatigue, awakens the thought and prevents drowsiness.

LU YU

WINE, SPIRITS, AND DRINKING

One reason why I don't drink is because I wish to know when I'm having a good time.

NANCY ASTOR

❖

The best audience is one that is intelligent, well-educated—and a little drunk.

ALBEN W. BARKLEY

Drinking makes such fools of people, and people are such fools to begin with, that it's compounding a felony.

ROBERT BENCHLEY

A man hath no better thing under the sun, than to eat, and to drink, and to be merry.

THE BIBLE (ECCLESIASTES 8:15)

TEETOTALER, n. One who abstains from strong drink, sometimes totally, sometimes tolerably totally.

AMBROSE BIERCE

When you stop drinking, you have to deal with this marvelous personality that started you drinking in the first place.

JIMMY BRESLIN

Alcohol is the prince of liquids and carries the palate to its highest pitch of exaltation.

A meal without wine is like a day without sunshine.

Burgundy makes you think of silly things; Bordeaux makes you talk about them, and Champagne makes you do them.

ANTHELME BRILLAT-SAVARIN

Then trust me, there's nothing like drinking
So pleasant on this side the grave;
It keeps the unhappy from thinking,
And makes e'en the valiant more brave.

CHARLES DIBDIN

Alcohol is necessary for a man so that he can have a good opinion of himself, undisturbed by the facts.

FINLEY PETER DUNNE

God made yeast, as well as dough, and loves fermentation just as dearly as he loves vegetation.

A man will be eloquent if you give him good wine.

There is this to be said in favor of drinking, that it takes the drunkard first out of society, then out of the world.

RALPH WALDO EMERSON

Temperance is the control of all the functions of our bodies. The man who refuses liquor, goes in for apple pie and develops a paunch, is no ethical leader for me.

JOHN ERSKINE

How gracious those dews of solace that over my senses fall
At the clink of the ice in the pitcher the boy brings up the hall.

EUGENE FIELD

Reminds me of my safari in Africa. Somebody forgot the corkscrew and for several days we had to live on nothing but food and water.

I never drink water. I'm afraid it will become habit-forming.

W. C. FIELDS

First you take a drink, then the drink takes a drink, then the drink takes you.

F. SCOTT FITZGERALD

Take counsel in wine, but resolve afterwards in water.

He that drinks fast, pays slow.

BENJAMIN FRANKLIN

Wine is earth's answer to the sun.

MARGARET FULLER

Wine is sunlight, held together by water.

GALILEO GALILEI

If wine tells truth—and so have said the wise,—
It makes me laugh to think how brandy lies!

OLIVER WENDELL HOLMES

Nothing ever tasted better than a cold beer on a beautiful afternoon with nothing to look forward to but more of the same.

HUGH HOOD

For it's always fair weather
When good fellows get together,
With a stein on the table and a good song ringing clear.

RICHARD HOVEY

Wine: An infallible antidote to commonsense and seriousness; an excuse for deeds otherwise unforgivable.

ELBERT HUBBARD

Those who drink beer will think beer.

WASHINGTON IRVING

I like liquor—its taste and its effects—and that is just the reason why I never drink it.

STONEWALL JACKSON

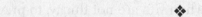

We drink one another's health and spoil our own.

JEROME K. JEROME

Wine gives great pleasure, and every pleasure is of itself a good.

SAMUEL JOHNSON

Even though a number of people have tried, no one has yet found a way to drink for a living.

JEAN KERR

Drink! for you know not whence you came nor why:
Drink! for you know not why you go, nor where.

OMAR KHAYYAM

The telephone is a good way to talk to people without having to offer them a drink.

FRAN LEBOWITZ

Only Irish coffee provides in a single glass all four essential food groups: alcohol, caffeine, sugar, and fat.

ALEX LEVINE

When you ask one friend to dine,
Give him your best wine!
When you ask two,
The second best will do!

HENRY WADSWORTH LONGFELLOW

I've made it a rule never to drink by daylight and never to refuse a drink after dark.

H. L. MENCKEN

One more drink and I'll be under the host.

DOROTHY PARKER

Wine is the most healthful and most hygienic of beverages.

LOUIS PASTEUR

There are two reasons for drinking; one is, when you are thirsty, to cure it; the other, when you are not thirsty, to prevent it . . . Prevention is better than cure.

THOMAS LOVE PEACOCK

Come quickly, I am tasting stars!

DOM PÉRIGNON, *on his discovery of champagne*

In vino veritas. (In wine there is truth.)

PLINY THE ELDER

Alcohol is a good preservative for everything but brains.

MARY PETTIBONE POOLE

❖

There are more old drunkards than old physicians.

FRANCOIS RABELAIS

❖

Alcohol is the anesthesia by which we endure the operation of life.

GEORGE BERNARD SHAW

❖

Wine is bottled poetry.

ROBERT LOUIS STEVENSON

❖

An alcoholic is someone you don't like who drinks as much as you do.

DYLAN THOMAS

❖

Sometimes too much to drink is barely enough.

MARK TWAIN

❖

It was my Uncle George who discovered that alcohol was a food well in advance of modern medical thought.

P. G. WODEHOUSE

❖

My grandmother is over eighty and still doesn't need glasses. Drinks right out of the bottle.

When I read about the evils of drinking, I gave up reading.

HENNY YOUNGMAN

COOKING

The fact is that it takes more than ingredients and technique to cook a good meal. A good cook puts something of *himself* into the preparation—he cooks with enjoyment, anticipation, spontaneity, and he is willing to experiment.

PEARL BAILEY

When compelled to cook, I produce a meal that would make a sword swallower gag.

RUSSELL BAKER

A gourmet who thinks of calories is like a tart who looks at her watch.

I don't like gourmet cooking or "this" cooking or "that" cooking. I like "good" cooking.

When I come home to my kitchen, I realize it is there that I can best satisfy the eccentricities of my own palate.

JAMES BEARD

I feel a recipe is only a theme, which an intelligent cook can play each time with a variation.

MADAME JEHANE BENOIT

Another cannot make fit to eat without wine or brandy. A third must have brandy on her apple dumplings, and a fourth comes out boldly and says she likes to drink once in a while herself too well. What flimsy excuses these! brandy and apple dumplings forsooth! That lady must be a wretched cook indeed who cannot make apple dumplings, mince pie, or cake palatable without the addition of poisonous substances.

AMELIA JENKS BLOOMER

Cookery is not chemistry. It is an art. It requires instinct and taste rather than exact measurements.

MARCEL BOULESTIN

Anyone who eats three meals a day should understand why cookbooks outsell sex books three to one.

L. M. BOYD

The discovery of a new dish does more for human happiness than the discovery of a new star.

Poultry is for the cook what canvas is for the painter.

ANTHELME BRILLAT-SAVARIN

Tomatoes and oregano make it Italian; wine and tarragon make it French. Sour cream makes it Russian; lemon and cinnamon make it Greek. Soy sauce makes it Chinese; garlic makes it good.

ALICE MAY BROCK

I don't even butter my bread. I consider that cooking.

KATHERINE CEBRIAN

Music with dinner is an insult both to the cook and to the violinist.

G. K. CHESTERTON

Too many cooks may spoil the broth, but it only takes one to burn it.

I was 32 when I started cooking; up until then, I just ate.

On nouvelle cuisine:
It's so beautifully arranged on the plate—you know someone's fingers have been all over it.

Non-cooks think it's silly to invest two hours' work in two minutes' enjoyment, but if cooking is evanescent, well, so is the ballet.

JULIA CHILD

❖

Sour, sweet, bitter, pungent—all must be tasted.

CHINESE PROVERB

❖

When she goes about her kitchen duties, chopping, carving, mixing, whisking, she moves with the grace and precision of a ballet dancer, her fingers plying the food with the dexterity of a croupier.

Cooking is at once child's play and adult joy. And cooking done with care is an act of love.

CRAIG CLAIBORNE

❖

As he chops, cuts, slices, trims, shapes, or threads through the string, a butcher is as good a sight to watch as a dancer or a mime.

COLETTE

❖

Life is too short to stuff a mushroom.

SHIRLEY CONRAN

Salt is the policeman of taste: it keeps the various flavors of a dish in order, and restrains the stronger from tyrannizing over the weaker.

MALCOLM DE CHAZAL

It does not matter whether one paints a picture, writes a poem, or carves a statue, simplicity is the mark of a master-hand. Don't run away with the idea that it is easy to cook simply. It requires a long apprenticeship.

ELSIE DE WOLFE

Progress in civilization has been accompanied by progress in cookery.

FANNIE FARMER

A watched pot never boils.

ELIZABETH GASKELL

Too many cooks spoil the broth.

SIR BALTHAZAR GERBIER

❖

Cooking is an art, but you eat it too.

MARCELLA HAZAN

❖

Condiments are like old friends—highly thought of, but often taken for granted.

MARILYN KAYTOR

❖

If you like good food, cook it yourself.

LI LIWENG

The fat in meat, fish, ducks and chicken must be kept in the meat and not allowed to run out, else the flavor is all in the juices.

YUAN MEI

Anybody can make you enjoy the first bite of a dish, but only a real chef can make you enjoy the last.

FRANCOIS MINOT

When you become a good cook, you become a good craftsman, first. You repeat and repeat and repeat until your hands know how to move without thinking about it.

JACQUES PEPIN

Many dishes bring many diseases.

PLINY THE ELDER

The two biggest sellers in any bookstore are the cookbooks and the diet books. The cookbooks tell you how to prepare the food and the diet books tell you how not to eat any of it.

ANDY ROONEY

A good cook is like a sorceress who dispenses happiness.

ELSA SCHIAPARELLI

If you are surprised at the number of our maladies, count our cooks.

SENECA

Epicurean cooks sharpen with cloyless sauce his appetite.

WILLIAM SHAKESPEARE

When men reach their sixties and retire, they go to pieces. Women go right on cooking.

GAIL SHEEHY

The most remarkable thing about my mother is that for thirty years she served the family nothing but leftovers. The original meal has never been found.

CALVIN TRILLIN

Cooking is like love. It should be entered into with abandon or not at all.

HARRIET VAN HORNE

From morning till night, sounds drift from the kitchen, most of them familiar and comforting. . . . On days when warmth is the most important need of the human heart, the kitchen is the place you can find it; it dries the wet sock, it cools the hot little brain.

E. B. WHITE

Garnishing of dishes has also a great deal to do with the appearance of a dinner-table, each dish garnished sufficiently to be in good taste without looking absurd.

HUGO ZIEMANN AND MRS. F. L. GILLETTE

DIETING

I'm on a seafood diet. I see food and I eat it.

ANONYMOUS

When it comes to eating, you can sometimes help yourself more by helping yourself less.

RICHARD ARMOUR

I've been on a diet for two weeks and all I've lost is two weeks.

TOTIE FIELDS

A diet is when you watch what you eat and wish you could eat what you watch.

HERMIONE GINGOLD

The second day of a diet is always easier than the first. By the second day you're off it.

JACKIE GLEASON

If you wish to grow thinner, diminish your dinner.

H. S. LEIGH

I told my doctor I get very tired when I go on a diet, so he gave me pep pills. Know what happened? I ate faster.

JOE E. LEWIS

An airline is a great place to diet.

WOLFGANG PUCK

But if one doesn't have a character like Abraham Lincoln or Joan of Arc, a diet simply disintegrates into eating exactly what you want to eat, but with a bad conscience.

MARIA AUGUSTA TRAPP

EATING

Nature delights in the most plain and simple diet. Every animal, but man, keeps to one dish.

JOSEPH ADDISON

Eat before shopping. If you go to the store hungry, you are likely to make unnecessary purchases.

AMERICAN HEART ASSOCIATION COOKBOOK

You are what you eat.

AMERICAN SAYING

Eat, drink, and be merry, for tomorrow we may diet.

ANONYMOUS

If the people have no bread, let them eat cake.

MARIE ANTOINETTE (attributed)

Before eating, always take time to thank the food.

ARAPAHO PROVERB

You don't get ulcers from what you eat. You get them from what's eating you.

VICKI BAUM

Why so many different dishes? Man sinks almost to the level of an animal when eating becomes his chief pleasure.

LUDWIG VON BEETHOVEN

Let us eat and drink; for tomorrow we shall die.

THE BIBLE (ISAIAH 22:13)

I am not a glutton—I am an explorer of food.

ERMA BOMBECK

Tell me what you eat, and I will tell you what you are.

Gluttony is mankind's exclusive prerogative.

He who eats too much knows not how to eat.

Animals feed, man eats; the man of intellect alone knows how to eat.

In compelling man to eat that he may live, Nature gives an appetite to invite him, and pleasure to reward him.

ANTHELME BRILLAT-SAVARIN

Now if you're ready, Oysters, dear, we can begin to feed!

LEWIS CARROLL

I eat at this German-Chinese restaurant and the food is delicious. The only problem is that an hour later you're hungry for power.

DICK CAVETT

Society is composed of two great classes—those who have more dinners than appetite, and those who have more appetite than dinners.

NICOLAS DE CHAMFORT

Just enough food and drink should be taken to restore our strength, and not to overburden it.

CICERO

Your eyes are always bigger than your stomach.

CONFUCIUS

The predominance of grease in the American kitchen, coupled with the habits of hearty eating, and constant expectoration, are the causes of the diseases of the stomach which are so common in America.

JAMES FENIMORE COOPER

If you are a rich man, eat whenever you please; and if you are a poor man, eat whenever you can.

DIOGENES THE CYNIC

He needs no more than birds and beasts to think,
All his occasions are to eat and drink.

JOHN DRYDEN

Nothing will benefit human health and increase chances for survival of life on Earth as much as the evolution to a vegetarian diet.

ALBERT EINSTEIN

❖

Taking food and drink is a great enjoyment for healthy people, and those who do not enjoy eating seldom have much capacity for enjoyment or usefulness of any sort.

CHARLES W. ELIOT

❖

Let the stoics say what they please, we do not eat for the good of living, but because the meat is savory and the appetite is keen.

RALPH WALDO EMERSON

❖

When I get a little money, I buy books. And if there is any left over, I buy food.

DESIDERIUS ERASMUS

❖

Once, during Prohibition, I was forced to live for days on nothing but food and water.

W. C. FIELDS

❖

In America we eat, collectively, with a glum urge for food to fill us. We are ignorant of flavour. We are as a nation taste-blind.

There are many of us who cannot but feel dismal about the future of various cultures. Often it is hard not to agree that we are becoming culinary nitwits, dependent upon fast foods and mass kitchens and megavitamins for our basically rotten nourishment.

M. F. K. FISHER

Eat to live, and not live to eat.

To lengthen thy life, lessen thy meals.

What one relishes, nourishes.

If, after exercise, we feed sparingly, the digestion will be easy and good, the body lightsome, the temper cheerful, and all the animal functions performed agreeably.

I saw few die of hunger; of eating, a hundred thousand.

Eat not to dullness; drink not to elevation.

In general, mankind, since the improvement of cookery, eats twice as much as nature requires.

BENJAMIN FRANKLIN

Glutton: one who digs his grave with his teeth.

Appetite comes with eating; the more one has, the more one would have.

FRENCH PROVERB

As a child my family's menu consisted of two choices: take it or leave it.

BUDDY HACKETT

There is small danger of being starved in our land of plenty; but the danger of being stuffed is imminent.

SARAH JOSEPHA HALE

On Howard Hughes:
One day when he was eating a cookie he offered me a bite. Don't underestimate that. The poor guy's so frightened of germs, it could darn near have been a proposal.

JEAN HARLOW

❖

One laughs when joyous, sulks when angry, is at peace with the world when the stomach is satisfied.

HAWAIIAN PROVERB

❖

Great eaters and great sleepers are incapable of anything else that is great.

HENRY IV OF FRANCE

❖

All things require skill but an appetite.

GEORGE HERBERT

❖

Better is half a loaf than no bread.

JOHN HEYWOOD

Eating while seated makes one of large size; eating while standing makes one strong.

HINDU PROVERB

More people will die from hit-or-miss eating than from hit-and-run driving.

DUNCAN HINES

In order to know whether a human being is young or old, offer it food of different kinds at short intervals. If young, it will eat anything at any hour of the day or night. If old, it observes stated periods.

OLIVER WENDELL HOLMES

Where the guests at a gathering are well-acquainted, they eat 20 percent more than they otherwise would.

EDGAR WATSON HOWE

If you ever have to support a flagging conversation, introduce the topic of eating.

LEIGH HUNT

Statistics show that of those who contract the habit of eating, very few survive.

WALLACE IRWIN

Before good food goes to waste, one should overeat.

JAMAICAN PROVERB

❖

A man shouldn't send away his plate till he has eaten his fill.

HENRY JAMES

❖

We never repent of having eaten too little.

THOMAS JEFFERSON

In a restaurant choose a table near a waiter.

One man has no appetite for his food, while another has no food for his appetite.

Only from your own table can you go away full.

He that eats till he is sick must fast till he is well.

JEWISH PROVERB

Some people have a foolish way of not minding, or pretending not to mind, what they eat. For my part, I mind my belly very studiously, and very carefully; for I look upon it, that he who does not mind his belly, will hardly mind anything else.

SAMUEL JOHNSON

When we lose, I eat. When we win, I eat. I also eat when we're rained out.

TOMMY LASORDA, *former manager, Los Angeles Dodgers*

That's something I've noticed about food: whenever there's a crisis if you can get people to eating normally things get better.

MADELEINE L'ENGLE

In America, a parent puts food in front of a child and says, "Eat it, it's good for you." In Europe, the parent says, "Eat it, it's good!"

JOHN LEVEE

Work before eating, rest after eating. Eat not ravenously, filling the mouth gulp after gulp without breathing space.

MAIMONIDES

Americans can eat garbage, provided you sprinkle it liberally with ketchup, mustard, chili sauce, Tabasco sauce, cayenne pepper, or any other condiment which destroys the original flavor of the dish.

HENRY MILLER

Isn't there any other part of the matzo you can eat?

MARILYN MONROE, *on being served matzo ball soup three meals in a row*

A true gastronome should always be ready to eat, just as a soldier should always be ready to fight.

CHARLES MONSELET

Stop short of your appetite; eat less than you are able.

OVID

One of the very nicest things about life is the way we must regularly stop whatever it is we are doing and devote our attention to eating.

LUCIANO PAVAROTTI

If thou rise with an appetite, thou art sure never to sit down without one.

WILLIAM PENN

Ecstasy is a glass of tea and a piece of sugar in the mouth.

ALEXANDER PUSHKIN

Appetite comes with eating . . . but thirst goes away with drinking.

FRANCOIS RABELAIS

❖

The appetite is sharpened by the first bites.

JOSE RIZAL

❖

It is not the horse that draws the cart, but the oats.

RUSSIAN PROVERB

❖

When the stomach is full, it is easy to talk of fasting.

SAINT JEROME

❖

Eating is not merely a material pleasure. Eating well gives a spectacular joy to life and contributes immensely to goodwill and happy companionship. It is of great importance to the morale.

ELSA SCHIAPARELLI

❖

To be always intending to live a new life, but never find time to set about it—this is as if a man should put off eating and drinking from one day to another till he be starved and destroyed.

SIR WALTER SCOTT

❖

What is nourishment to a hungry man becomes a burden to a full stomach.

SENECA

❖

Things sweet to taste prove in digestion sour.

Do as adversaries in law, strive mightily,
But eat and drink as friends.

Who riseth from a feast
With that keen appetite that he sits down?

With eager feeding, food doth choke the feeder.

He hath eaten me out of house and home.

What is a man
If his chief good and market of his time
Be but to sleep and feed?
A beast, no more.

WILLIAM SHAKESPEARE

Everything I eat has been proved by some doctor or other to be
a deadly poison, and everything I don't eat has been proved to be
indispensable to life. . . . But I go marching on.

GEORGE BERNARD SHAW

I eat merely to put food out of my mind.

N. F. SIMPSON

If you are looking for a fly in your food it means that you are
full.

SOUTH AFRICAN PROVERB

❖

Give me a fish, I eat for a day. Teach me to fish, I eat for a life-
time.

ROBERT LOUIS STEVENSON

Success to me is having ten honeydew melons, and eating only the top half of each one.

BARBRA STREISAND

❖

'Tis not the meat, but 'tis the appetite
Makes eating a delight.

SIR JOHN SUCKLING

❖

In eating, a third of the stomach should be filled with food, a third with drink, and the rest left empty.

THE TALMUD

❖

A fully gorged belly never produced a sprightly mind.

JEREMY TAYLOR

❖

He who distinguishes the true savor of his food can never be a glutton; he who does not cannot be otherwise.

I have no doubt that it is a part of the destiny of the human race, in its gradual improvement, to leave off eating animals.

Live in each season as it passes; breathe the air, drink the drink, taste the fruit, and resign yourself to the influences of each.

HENRY DAVID THOREAU

❖

Seeing is deceiving. It's eating that's believing.

JAMES THURBER

To eat is human
To digest divine.

Part of the secret of success in life is to eat what you like and let the food fight it out inside.

MARK TWAIN

Life is uncertain. Eat dessert first.

ERNESTINE ULMER

Strength is the capacity to break a chocolate bar into four pieces with your bare hands—and then eat just one of the pieces.

JUDITH VIORST

Nothing would be more tiresome than eating and drinking if God had not made them a pleasure as well as a necessity.

VOLTAIRE

In our opinion food should be sniffed lustily at table, both as a matter of precaution and as a matter of enjoyment, the sniffing of it to be regarded in the same light as the tasting of it.

E. B. WHITE

Have we not stood here like trees in the ground long enough? Have we not groveled here long enough, eating and drinking like mere brutes?

WALT WHITMAN

When I am in trouble, eating is the only thing that consoles me. Indeed, when I am really in great trouble, as anyone who knows me intimately will tell you, I refuse everything except food and drink.

OSCAR WILDE

FOODS

One man's poison ivy is another man's spinach.

GEORGE ADE

A crust eaten in peace is better than a banquet partaken in anxiety.

AESOP

He dreamed he was eating shredded wheat and woke up to find the mattress half gone.

FRED ALLEN

Those who forget the pasta are condemned to reheat it.

ANONYMOUS

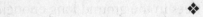

Though they could not all talk, they could all eat; and the beautiful pyramids of grapes, nectarines and peaches soon collected them around the table.

JANE AUSTEN

The French fried potato has become an inescapable horror in almost every public eating place in the country. "French fries," say the menus, but they are not French fries any longer. They are a furry-textured substance with the taste of plastic wood.

RUSSELL BAKER

Eating rice cakes is like chewing on a foam coffee cup, only less filling.

DAVE BARRY

I would like to find a stew that will give me heartburn immediately, instead of at three o'clock in the morning.

JOHN BARRYMORE

Food is our common ground, a universal experience.

Good bread is the most fundamentally satisfying of all foods; and good bread with fresh butter, the greatest of feasts.

JAMES BEARD

The bagel is a lonely roll to eat all by yourself because in order for the true taste to come out you need your family. One to cut the bagels, one to toast them, one to put on the cream cheese and the lox, one to put them on the table and one to supervise.

GERTRUDE BERG

TURKEY, n. A large bird whose flesh when eaten on certain religious anniversaries has the peculiar property of attesting piety and gratitude. Incidentally, it is pretty good eating.

EDIBLE, adj. Good to eat, and wholesome to digest, as a worm to a toad, a toad to a snake, a snake to a pig, a pig to a man, and a man to a worm.

AMBROSE BIERCE

I prefer my oysters fried;
That way I know my oysters died.

ROY G. BLOUNT, JR.

Research tells us that fourteen out of any ten individuals like chocolate.

SANDRA BOYNTON

On the plain household bread his eye did not dwell; but he surveyed with favor some currant tea-cakes, and condescended to make choice of one.

CHARLOTTE BRONTË

❖

I doubt the world holds for anyone a more soul-stirring surprise than the first adventure with ice cream.

HEYWOOD BROUN

❖

That last cherry soothes a roughness of my palate.

If thou tastest a crust of bread, thou tastest all the stars and all the heavens.

ROBERT BROWNING

❖

Food for all is a necessity. Food should not be a merchandise, to be bought and sold as jewels are bought and sold by those who have the money to buy. Food is a human necessity, like water and air, and it should be available.

PEARL BUCK

❖

Always eat grapes downward—that is eat the best grapes first; in this way there will be none better left on the bunch, and each grape will seem good down to the last. If you eat the other way, you will not have a good grape in the lot.

SAMUEL BUTLER

Food, one assumes, provides nourishment; but Americans eat it fully aware that small amounts of poison have been added to improve its appearance and delay its putrefaction.

JOHN CAGE

Beautiful soup! Who cares for fish,
Game, or any other dish?
Who would not give all else for two
Pennyworth of beautiful soup?

LEWIS CARROLL

Watermelon—it's a good fruit,
You eat, you drink, you wash your face.

ENRICO CARUSO

It is impossible to read English novels without realizing how important a part food plays in the mental as in the physical life of the Englishman.

ELISABETH LUTHER CARY

An herb is the friend of physicians and the praise of cooks.

CHARLEMAGNE

Well loved he garlic, onions, and eke leeks,
And for to drinken strong wine, red as blood.

GEOFFREY CHAUCER

Poets have been mysteriously silent on the subject of cheese.

G. K. CHESTERTON

When they talk about healthy food, they usually mean things that don't taste very good.

Fake food—I mean those patented substances chemically flavored and mechanically bulked out to kill the appetite and deceive the gut—is unnatural, almost immoral, a bane to good eating and good cooking.

I just hate health food.

JULIA CHILD

❖

Pistachio nuts, the red ones, cure any problem.

PAULA DANZIGER

❖

It breathes reassurance, it offers consolation; after a weary day it promotes sociability. . . . There is nothing like a bowl of hot soup . . .

LOUIS DEGOUY

❖

The coffee was boiling over a charcoal fire, and large slices of bread and butter were piled one upon the other like deals in a lumber yard.

CHARLES DICKENS

❖

I did not know the ample bread,
'T was so unlike the crumb
The birds and I had often shared
In Nature's dining-room.

EMILY DICKINSON

❖

Wine is the intellectual part of a meal while meat is the material.

ALEXANDRE DUMAS

There are only ten minutes in the life of a pear when it is perfect to eat.

RALPH WALDO EMERSON

❖

One man's meat is another man's poison.

Butter is gold in the morning, silver at noon, and lead at night.

ENGLISH PROVERB

❖

Plain fare gives as much pleasure as a costly diet, while bread and water confer the highest possible pleasure when they are brought to hungry lips.

EPICURUS

❖

Cheese—milk's leap toward immortality.

CLIFTON FADIMAN

❖

The bagel, an unsweetened doughnut with rigor mortis . . .

BEATRICE AND IRA FREEMAN

Don't get any dainties for me, my dear; bread and cheese is the chief of my diet.

I'll make her a pudding, and a pudding she'll like, too. . . .

Many a one has been comforted in their sorrow by seeing a good dish come upon the table.

ELIZABETH GASKELL

Food is the most primitive form of comfort.

SHEILAH GRAHAM

The soup, thin and dark and utterly savorless, tasted as if it had been drained out of the umbrella stand.

MARGARET HALSEY

Never blow your soup if it is too hot, but wait until it cools. Never raise your plate to your lips, but eat with your spoon.

C. B. HARTLEY

Of all smells, bread; of all tastes, salt.

GEORGE HERBERT

Let food be your medicine and medicine be your food.

HIPPOCRATES

Conversation is the enemy of good wine and food.

ALFRED HITCHCOCK

There is something in the red of a raspberry pie that looks as good to a man as the red in a sheep looks to a wolf.

EDGAR WATSON HOWE

Laughter is brightest, in the place where the food is.

IRISH PROVERB

I don't like to eat snails. I prefer fast food.

STRANGE DE JIM

❖

A cucumber should be well-sliced, dressed with pepper and vinegar, and then thrown out.

SAMUEL JOHNSON

❖

Talking of Pleasure, this moment I was writing with one hand and with the other holding to my Mouth a Nectarine—good God how fine. It went down soft, pulpy, slushy, oozy—all its delicious embodiment melted down my throat like a large Beautiful strawberry.

JOHN KEATS

Food for thought is no substitute for the real thing.

WALT KELLY

❖

It requires a certain kind of mind to see beauty in a hamburger bun.

RAY KROC, *founder of McDonald's*

If we do not permit the earth to produce beauty and joy, it will in the end not produce food either.

JOSEPH WOOD KRUTCH

❖

There is a physiognomical character in the taste for food. C— holds that a man cannot have a pure mind who refuses apple-dumplings.

CHARLES LAMB

Food is an important part of a balanced diet.

Vegetables are interesting but lack a sense of purpose when unaccompanied by a good cut of meat.

Large, naked, raw carrots are acceptable as food only to those who live in hutches eagerly awaiting Easter.

Cold soup is a very tricky thing and it is a rare hostess who can carry it off. More often than not the dinner guest is left with the impression that had he only come a little earlier he could have gotten it while it was still hot.

FRAN LEBOWITZ

❖

Vegetarian: A person who eats only side dishes.

GERALD LIEBERMAN

❖

Everything you see I owe to spaghetti.

SOPHIA LOREN

❖

What is food to one is to another bitter poison.

LUCRETIUS

❖

The trouble with eating Italian food is that 5 or 6 days later you're hungry again.

GEORGE MILLER

❖

You can travel fifty thousand miles in America without once tasting a piece of good bread.

HENRY MILLER

It's good food and not fine words that keeps me alive.

MOLIÈRE

No man is alone while eating spaghetti—it requires so much attention.

ROBERT MORLEY

Fine words do not produce food.

NIGERIAN PROVERB

A nickel will get you on the subway, but garlic will get you a seat.

OLD NEW YORK PROVERB

Old people shouldn't eat health foods. They need all the preservatives they can get.

I understand the big food companies are developing a tearless onion. I think they can do it—after all, they've already given us tasteless bread.

ROBERT ORBEN

I never had a piece of toast
Particularly long and wide,
But fell upon the sanded floor,
And always on the buttered side.

JAMES PAYN

Fish, to taste right, must swim three times—in water, in butter, and in wine.

POLISH PROVERB

No man in the world has more courage than the man who can stop after eating one peanut.

CHANNING POLLACK

An apple a day keeps the doctor away.

PROVERB

Our minds are like our stomachs; they are whetted by the change of their food, and variety supplies both with fresh appetites.

MARCUS FABIUS QUINTILLIAN

You can tell a lot about a fellow's character by his way of eating jellybeans.

RONALD REAGAN

Health food may be good for the conscience but Oreos taste a hell of a lot better.

ROBERT REDFORD

A bagel is a doughnut with the sin removed.

GEORGE ROSENBAUM

It is a fact that great eaters of meat are in general more cruel and ferocious than other men.

JEAN JACQUES ROUSSEAU

Bread and butter, devoid of charm in the drawing-room, is ambrosia eating under a tree.

ELIZABETH RUSSELL

I am a great eater of beef, and I believe that does harm to my wit.

Give them great meals of beef and iron and steel, they will eat like wolves and fight like devils.

. . . eat no onions nor garlic, for we are to utter sweet breath.

WILLIAM SHAKESPEARE

Let onion atoms lurk within the bowl
And, half suspected, animate the whole.

SYDNEY SMITH

The only emperor is the emperor of ice-cream.

WALLACE STEVENS

Fish is eaten with an ordinary fork, with as much dexterity in the evasion of bones as can be commanded with such an inadequate instrument, and a bit of bread as an aid.

FREDERICK A. STOKES

Bread is the staff of life.

JONATHAN SWIFT

❖

Food is better than drink up to the age of forty; after forty, drink is better.

THE TALMUD

I never was much of an oyster eater, nor can I relish them *in naturalibus* as some do, but require a quantity of sauces, lemons, cayenne peppers, bread and butter, and so forth, to render them palatable.

Presently, we were aware of an odour gradually coming towards us, something musky, fiery, savoury, mysterious,—a hot drowsy smell, that lulls the senses, and yet enflames them,—the *truffles* were coming.

WILLIAM MAKEPEACE THACKERAY

When it comes to Chinese food I have always operated under the policy that the less known about the preparation the better. . . . A wise diner who is invited to visit the kitchen replies by saying, as politely as possible, that he has a pressing engagement.

CALVIN TRILLIN

When one has tasted watermelon he knows what the angels eat.

Cauliflower is nothing but cabbage with a college education.

MARK TWAIN

Lettuce is like conversation: it must be fresh and crisp, and so sparkling that you scarcely notice the bitter in it.

CHARLES DUDLEY WARNER

To a waiter:
When I ask for a watercress sandwich, I do not mean a loaf with a field in the middle of it.

To make a good salad is to be a brilliant diplomat—to know how much oil to put with one's vinegar.

OSCAR WILDE

The first time I ate organic whole-grain bread I swear it tasted like roofing material.

ROBIN WILLIAMS

We [the Chinese] eat food for its texture, the elastic or crisp effect it has on our teeth, as well as for fragrance, flavor and color.

LIN YUTANG

FOOD AND LOVE

Men become passionately attached to women who know how to cosset them with delicate tidbits.

HONORÉ DE BALZAC

The most important things to do in the world are to get something to eat, something to drink and somebody to love you.

BRENDAN BEHAN

Sustain me with raisins, refresh me with apples; for I am sick with love.

THE BIBLE (SONG OF SOLOMON 2:5)

Happy and successful cooking doesn't rely only on know-how; it comes from the heart, makes great demands on the palate and needs enthusiasm and a deep love of food to bring it to life.

GEORGES BLANC

I'm at the age where food has taken the place of sex in my life. In fact, I've just had a mirror put over my kitchen table.

RODNEY DANGERFIELD

❖

The way to a man's heart is through his stomach.

FANNY FERN

❖

Sharing food with another human being is an intimate act that should not be indulged in lightly.

Our three basic needs for food and security and love are so mixed and mingled and entwined that we cannot straightly think of one without the other.

M. F. K. FISHER

❖

There is one thing more exasperating than a wife who can cook and won't and that's a wife who can't cook and will.

ROBERT FROST

❖

Of soup and love, the first is the best.

THOMAS FULLER

❖

We are taught that man most loves and admires the domestic type of woman. This is one of the roaring jokes of history. The breakers of hearts, the queens of romance, the goddesses of a thousand devotees, have not been cooks.

CHARLOTTE PERKINS GILMAN

❖

Kissing don't last: cookery do!

GEORGE MEREDITH

There is no sincerer love than the love of food.

GEORGE BERNARD SHAW

[Some] Chinese mothers show they love their children, not through hugs and kisses, but with stern offerings of steamed dumplings.

AMY TAN

There is no spectacle on earth more appealing than that of a beautiful woman in the act of cooking dinner for someone she loves.

THOMAS WOLFE

HUNGER

Hunger makes you restless. You dream about food—not just any food, but perfect food, the best food, magical meals, famous and awe-inspiring, the one piece of meat, the exact taste of buttery corn, tomatoes so ripe they split and sweeten the air, beans so crisp they snap between the teeth, gravy like mother's milk singing to your bloodstream.

DOROTHY ALLISON

Hunger knows no friend but its feeder.

ARISTOPHANES

For I was hungered, and ye gave me meat: I was thirsty and ye gave me drink: I was a stranger, and ye took me in.

THE BIBLE (MATTHEW 25:35)

Hunger is the best sauce in the world.

MIGUEL DE CERVANTES

❖

No man can be a patriot on an empty stomach.

WILLIAM COWPER

❖

Of all diseases, hunger is the worst.

THE DHAMMAPADA

❖

A man is hungry all day long. A man is perpetually eating.

CHARLES DICKENS

❖

I had been hungry all the years;
My noon had come, to dine;
I, trembling, drew the table near,
And touched the curious wine.

EMILY DICKINSON

❖

An empty stomach is not a good political adviser.

ALBERT EINSTEIN

❖

I can reason down or deny everything, except this perpetual
Belly: feed he must and will, and I cannot make him respectable.

RALPH WALDO EMERSON

People ask me: "Why do you write about food, and eating, and drinking? Why don't you write about the struggle for power and security, and about love, the way the others do?" . . . The easiest answer is to say that, like most other humans, I am hungry.

When I write of hunger, I am really writing about love and the hunger for it, and warmth and the love of it . . . and it is all one.

M. F. K. FISHER

A hungry stomach has no ears.

JEAN DE LA FONTAINE

A good meal ought to begin with hunger.

FRENCH PROVERB

God comes to the hungry in the form of food.

MAHATMA GANDHI

Hunger is felt by a slave and hunger is felt by a king.

GHANAIAN PROVERB

Hunger can explain many acts. It can be said that all vile acts are done to satisfy hunger.

MAXIM GORKY

I would ask you now to let me eat. There is nothing more devoid of shame than the accursed belly; it thrusts itself upon a man's mind in spite of his afflictions, in spite of his inward grief. That is true of me; my heart is sad, but my belly keeps urging me to have food and drink, tries to blot out all the past from me; it says imperiously: "Eat and be filled."

A hungry stomach will not allow its owner to forget it, whatever his cares and sorrows.

HOMER

Only a stomach that rarely feels hungry scorns common food.

HORACE

A hungry man is an angry man.

JAMES HOWELL

> For nothing keeps a poet
> In his high singing mood
> Like unappeasable hunger
> For unattainable food.

JOYCE KILMER

An army marches on its stomach.

NAPOLEON

A good meal makes a man feel more charitable toward the whole world than any sermon.

ARTHUR PENDENYS

It is a hard matter, my fellow citizens, to argue with the belly, since it has no ears.

PLUTARCH

❖

The belly is ungrateful—it always forgets we already gave it something.

RUSSIAN PROVERB

❖

The brain may be important, but the stomach is still in charge!

CHARLES M. SCHULZ, *Peanuts* comic strip

❖

A great step toward independence is a good-humoured stomach.

SENECA

❖

With corn to make your needy bread,
And give them life whom hunger starved half dead.

WILLIAM SHAKESPEARE

❖

The body craves food only that the mind may think.

WILLIAM GILMORE SIMMS

❖

Plenty sits still, hunger is a wanderer.

SOUTH AFRICAN PROVERB

❖

I told him . . . that we ate when we were not hungry, and drank without the provocation of thirst.

JONATHAN SWIFT

My piece of bread only belongs to me when I know that everyone else has a share, and that no one starves while I eat.

LEO TOLSTOY

Principles have no real force except when one is well fed.

MARK TWAIN

Hunger: One of the few cravings that cannot be appeased with another solution.

IRWIN VAN GROVE